PROOF OF A SECRET GOVERNMENT

By

WICKLIFFE B. VENNARD, SR.

OMNI PUBLICATIONS
P.O. Box 216
Hawthorne, Calif. 90250

ISBN: 978-2-925369-09-7
Printed in the USA.

THE AUTHOR: —1968

WICKLIFFE B. VENNARD, SR.

Born June 16, 1900

Graduated Tulane University, 1921, in Mechanical and Electrical Engineering

Married to his College Chum for 41 years, has three Children and two Grandsons

Spent three years in the Development Engineering Department of Western Electric Co., Chicago, Ill.

From 1924 to date in the Life Insurance Field:

In 1931 ranked 6th out of 5500 Agents of Travelers Insurance Company

1932 to 1962 was Manager Houston Branch, Acacia Mutual Life Insurance Company. From 1962 to date acting as Agent for said Company

40 years in the Business Field aided the Author to understand and know how to research and analyze what is going on in the United States National Affairs

26 years spent endeavoring to alert the People of this Great Country to their jeopardy. During this period has spent all income above living expenses toward the cause of Christ and Country, all done as a Public Service to his Fellow Americans.

25¢ per copy, 10 or more copies 15¢ each.

The most powerful right that any government has is the right to issue and control its own money and credit.

We know of no government on the face of the earth today that has retained unto itself this right. Every government has given up its sovereignty, its birth-right, by delegating this all-powerful right to private corporations (monopolies) owned and controlled by International Bankers. They own and control all large news media and ether waves. We, of the so-called Free World, are led to believe that we have Constitutional, voting and other rights, which is simply not so. The only difference is this – those countries behind the Iron Curtain have had Blood Baths. The I.B.s control the entire world through the control of money.

Sixty years ago, Col. E. Mandel House laid down our blueprint for ruin in "Philip Dru - Administrator." Order from Rev. Kenneth Goff, 3406 South Bryant Street, Englewood, Colorado. The book was written as a novel, anonymously. Later Col. House admitted authorship. He apparently was a front man for the European I.B.s. He became the Advisor to President Wilson. By whose authority?

They well knew that President Taft would veto the Federal Reserve Act, so they "button-holed" the great dreamer, the college professor, Woodrow Wilson.

This book outlines the Plan of Action–1.) Federal Reserve System, 2.) World War I, 3.) League of Nations, 4.) Versailles Treaty, 5.) One-World Government.

All went like clock-work until the U.S. Senate refused to ratify the League of Nations. Wilson, House, et al., were in Paris making arrangements for the Versailles Treaty (1919) at the time.

House then organized the Council of Foreign Relations: S. W. corner of Park Avenue and 68th Street, N.Y.C. in order to re-initiate this Plan of Action. On the "second bounce," they put it over: 1.) Federal Reserve Act (already enacted), 2.) World War II, 3.) United Nations, 4.) Yalta Treaty, 5.) One-World Government.

When Wilson finally awakened, he said, "I am a most unhappy man; unwittingly I have ruined my country." He broke with Col. House and forbade him to come to his home, his office, or his funeral.

The C.F.R. (Establishment) headquarters are in N.Y.C. There are 29 organizations throughout the land. The great majority of the members are wealthy and prominent businessmen who are unaware of the behind-the-scenes machinations. If you wish to know the names of the members residing in your neighborhood, order "The Invisible Government," by Dan Smoot, 6551 Gaston Avenue, Dallas, Texas 75214, and order "Power Behind The Government Today," by Helen P. Lassell, from Omni Publications, Box 216, Hawthorne, California 90250 — and secure a June 1966 Esquire magazine from one of your subscriber friends. It has a four-page article entitled "The Wall Street Establishment" and contains a list of prominent citizens under the heading "The Invisible Empire."

In order to frame the people's minds for war, a planned "incident" was necessary. The "incident" for WW I was the assassination of the Archduke of Austria. The "incident" required for bringing the United States into the war was the sinking of the Lusitania. The "incident" for World War II was Pearl Harbor.

In this country the Establishment is known as the Secret Government or the Council on Foreign Relations; in Britain as the Royal Institute of International Affairs; and in Russia as the Communist Party.

For fifty years the C.F.R. has controlled both Major Parties in the U.S.A.; i.e., a one-party money Dictatorship. The pattern has been: either the Presidential or V.P. Candidate on both Tickets must be a C.F.R. member. We have been running to the polls for fifty years, thinking that we had a choice. Herbert Hoover, alone, fooled them; so they made him the scape-goat by means of the 1929 Crash. Those "in the know" got out of the market; $300 Million were taken out of circulation; and two Gold Shipments were made to France, thereby causing the ceiling to fall in.

What better proof does a citizen need, that the Republican Party is controlled, then when it refused to nominate Robert Taft and Gen. Douglas MacArthur in 1951. Then and there the Constitution Party was organized in Texas. Gen. MacArthur agreed to be the Presidential candidate. Arrangements were made for a parade in Houston, Texas, as well as his historic speech at the Rice Institute Stadium. The enemy, whoever they are, put out the propaganda "Listen on radio; you will be unable to get a seat." Sure enough, the attendance was not good. This incident evidently hurt the General deeply, for he walled himself up in the Waldorf Tower thereafter.

From 1952 to 1964 (inclusive) the Constitution Party of Texas never failed to comply with the rigid state regulations in fielding a complete slate of candidates. The fifteen planks in our platform were written to abolish the Federal Reserve Act as well as fourteen other deviations from our original Constitution and Bill of Rights, as laid down by the Founding Fathers.

Quote from Senate Document No. 23, 76th Congress, 1st session, p. 66:

Democratic national platform in 1932:

"We maintain that the depression of 1920 and the depression of 1929 were due to the indefensible contraction of credit for private profit at public expense and we pledge the Democratic Party to preserve a sound currency at all hazards. The Democratic candidates pledge their endorsement of this platform 100 percent. We promise to restore property values and to endeavor to establish a dollar of uniform permanent debt-paying power."

Democratic national platform in 1936:

"We approve the object of a permanent sound currency stablized so as to prevent the former wide fluctuations in value, injuring in turn, the producers, debtors, and property owners, on the one hand, and wage earners and creditors, on the other—a currency which will permit full utilization of the country's resources."

Republican national platform, 1932:

"We pledge a sound currency at all hazards. We will restore to the Congress the authority lodged with it by the Constitution to coin all money and regulate the value thereof."

Republican platform for 1936:

"We advocate a sound currency to be preserved at all hazards."

• • • •

"We will restore to the Congress the authority lodged with it by the Constitution to coin money and regulate the value thereof."

Progressive Party platform, 1938:

"The ownership and control of money and credit, without qualification or reservation, must be under

public and not private control."

Farmer Labor Party platform, 1934:

"Congress shall exercise the constitutional power to coin money and to regulate the value thereof."

(END OF QUOTE)

We were unsuccessful in our endeavors to draft Sen. Thurmond, Sen. Byrd, Gen. Walker and ex-Gov. Wallace. Our Committee for Wallace had secured 8,500 signatures in order to secure his ballot position. When he decided to run on the American Party ticket, we gave them the signatures. The Constitution Party of Texas decided to become autonomous; not field a slate of candidates; leaving the members to vote as they so desired. We feel that our Educational and Legal action on the restoration of Art. 1, Sec. 8, Par. 5, our only goal since 1938, as well as our Political action since 1951 brought many votes to the Wallace camp. Mr. Wallace did advise us that "he was behind us 100% in denouncing the FED; and we could quote him on that." We made voluminous mailings of that statement below his picture, coast to coast.

Richard Troxell, the Texas State Chairman of the Constitution Party, was nominated for President by North Dakota, and was placed on the ballot. NBC-TV invited all presidential and vice presidential candidates to speak on their Hollywood, California national hook-up. All spoke except Troxell. When they invited him by telephone, they asked what he was going to talk about. He advised that he would talk about the Federal Reserve System. They then advised that they would call back; but they never did.

The Constitution Party of Texas has revised its platform. The Preamble now states: "The Constitution Party of Texas re-affirms its belief in God and the inspiration of Jesus Christ as revealed in the

United States Constitution and its first ten amendments." The one and only plank provides for the restoration of Art. 1, Sec. 8, Par. 5, of the Constitution USA.

"Americans For America" is a nation-wide, nonpartisan organization with the same goal, using Educational and Legal means described herein.

After Sen. Strom Thurmond and Dean Manion orated for hours urging the audience to fight Communism, I had a few minutes with them. I advised thát they had accomplished nothing; might just as well tell the people to go out and fight a hurricane with fly swatters. We must cut off the water of the I.B.s, who finance Communism, by abolishing the Federal Reserve System. They both advised that "they knew nothing of the money issue."

Billy Graham and Dan Smoot were asked why they did not hit on the money issue. Both replied that "they knew nothing of the money issue."

Robert Welch and Tom Anderson (both J.B.S.) were asked if they had read Vennard's books. They both replied like poll-parrots, "Yes, but I don't go along with the thinking." That is the same thing as saying, they don't go along with the thinking of the Founding Fathers in laying down Art. 1, Sec. 8, Par. 5. None who make their living out of this fight for Christ and Country will touch the money issue.

I sent my Books, Alerts, Bills for Congress, the Joint Reolution for the State Legislatures, and copies of Legal Briefs to prove the un-Constitutionality of the F.R.S., to every member of Both House of Congress. I received one reply from Congressman Bob Casey, "No chance. No one here will touch the money issue." When McFadden, McCarran, and McCarthy died, Congress died.

Our Joint Resolution has been introduced in Arkansas, Mississippi, Minnesota and Idaho. We have assurance that it will be introduced in Alabama at the next session. All defeated.

Three Lawsuits have been tried in District Courts, and one in a Circuit Court of Appeals. It was also introduced in the House of Commons, England. All defeated. Read "The Solution to the Federal Reserve Fraud"—Omni Publications, P.O. Box 216, Hawthorne, California 90250 — 50¢.

Our Alert #19, "The Court of Last Resort" refers to Art. 3, Sec. 2, Par. 2 of the U.S. Constitution, which provides "All cases in which a state shall be a party, the U.S. Supreme Court shall have original jurisdiction." Will your Governor serve as a plaintiff?

We are also endeavoring to get ONE nation to start rolling back the carpet by issuing and controlling its own money and credit. As a start, we have been alerting the Vatican State, Spain, Portugal, Rhodesia, South Africa and the Indian Territories within the USA.

The following article appeared in the Houston Post, December 8, 1968:

PORTUGAL PLANS MONEY CHANGES

Lisbon—(UPI)—Portugal may soon make its own banknotes, currently produced in England and Holland according to Finance Minister Dias Rosas. Rosas also said the minting of 20, 30 and 35-escudo silver coins is under study. The coin of highest value now in circulation is of five escudos. An escudo is worth about 3.5 cents, U.S.

This is the greatest news since President Lincoln issued $450 million United States Notes in 1862. The thunder from this bomb-shell will reverberate around the globe. Portugal is the logical spot to begin rolling the carpet back. History has proved that they not only understand the behind-the-scenes intrigue of International Bankers, but they are fearless. Spain will be next because they alone defeated their hachet-men (the Bolsheviks).

The following quotes were made regarding the United States Notes issued by President Lincoln, in accordance with Art. 1, Sec. 8, Par. 5, of the Constitution:

"If that mischievous financial policy which had its origin in the North American republic during the Civil War in that country should become indurated down to a fixture, then that government will furnish its money without cost. It will pay off its debts and be without a debt. It will have all the money necessary to carry on its commerce. It will become prosperous beyond precedent in the history of the civilized governments of the world. The brains and wealth of all countries will go to North America. That government must be destroyed, or it will destroy every monarchy on this globe."—LONDON TIMES.

"If ever a monument should be erected to an inanimate object, then it should be erected in memory of the services of the United States notes—the 'greenbacks.' Such a monument would give us new courage and hope and would assist materially in bringing about a monetary system that would serve all the people and not just a few international manipulators."—SEN. WM. LEMKE.

"TREASURY DEPARTMENT, FISCAL SERVICE, WASHINGTON 25, D.C.
March 19, 1963

"The Honorable Wright Patman, Chairman
Banking and Currency Committee
House of Representatives
Washington 25, D.C.

"Dear Mr. Chairman:

"During Secretary Dillon's testimony before your Committee on the proposal to repeal certain silver legislation, you mentioned that a few years ago someone determined how much it would have cost the Government at 5 per cent interest to have borrowed the equivalent of United States notes which have been outstanding. ($346,000,000 outstanding since 1863. They are the Lincoln Greenbacks. W.P.) At your suggestion, Secretary Dillon offered to bring the figure up to date for you.

"The information which you recalled was possibly that contained in a letter addressed to you from the Treasury dated August 29, 1960, in reply to your request for that information in a letter dated December 13, 1934, signed by the Treasurer of the United States be brought up to date. The 1960 letter stated that if amounts equivalent to United States notes outstanding had borne interest at the rate of 5 per cent per annum, compounded semi-annually, the total interest cost through June 30, 1960, would have amounted to approximately $44 billion.

"Under the formula of the 1960 letter, the figure as of December 31, 1962, would exceed $49 billion.

"United States notes are carried in the statement of the public debt in the Daily Statement of the Treasury of the United States under the heading 'Debt Bearing No Interest.' For this purpose, however, from the amount outstanding there is deducted the amount of the gold reserve held for their redemption.

"It must always be recognized, of course, that the figures with which you have been supplied from time to time are purely hypothetical; not only were the 5 per cent rate of interest and the compounding of interest semi-annually merely assumed many years ago, but more importantly the figures have not taken account of the holding since the year 1900 of the gold reserve in excess of $150 million.

"Sincerely yours, John K. Carlock, Fiscal Assistant

Secretary."

1763—Benjamin Franklin was asked in London "why the Colonies had prospered so." He replied, "because we issue our own money."

1764—The prohibition by England against the New England colonies to issue their own currencies was now extended to the rest of the colonies.

1774—First Continental Congress met.

1775—The resulting chaos precipitated the Revolutionary War, according to Benjamin Franklin.

After World War I, Germany was defeated and destitute. The immediate change to prosperity and economic security was due to the fact that they issued and controlled their own money and credit.

Our Revolutionary War, the War of 1812, the Civil War, World War I and World War II were fomented by the I.B.s as a means of getting control of this nation's money and credit. Read Alert #1, "The Chronological History of United States Money" — Omni Publications — 25¢.

The Korean War and the Vietnam War were not "declared" by Congress. They are known as "Police Actions" or "United Nations Wars." The purpose is to further One-World Government.

The following articles from the Houston Post — 9-8-68 and 11-24-68 — will throw some light on the difficulties encountered in Third Party Political Action in Texas. These and other difficulties may prevail in other states.

Excerpts from the Houston Post — Sunday, September 8, 1968:

"Wallace Camp Stricken With 'Birchitis' by Brooks Keller, Post Reporter.

"It's not all sweetness and light under the political ten of George Wallace's presidential campaign in Texas.

"There is a growing division in the top rank of his

followers, caused mainly by the apparent heavy overlay of John Birch Society members on the state executive committee of Wallace's American Party.

"BARD LOGAN, state chairman of the American Party, admits readily that he's been a John Birch member for five years. Logan is a hardy perennial of right-wing, third-party politics in Texas.

His critics in and out of the American Party in Texas say that 27 or 28 out of 31 members of the party's executive committee are Birchers.

Logan says this estimate of Birch representation on the committee is too high, and adds that his critics are 'pathological Birch-haters.'

" 'I don't think Birch membership makes any difference in politics, and I don't intend to succumb to any campaign of Birch-haters,' Logan said.

"THREE OF LOGAN'S sternest critics are Temple businessmen Roy N. Lewellen and Carter Foster, and Albert W. Steele, a Waco public school teacher.

"They have established a separate office from the American Party in Temple. The new office is called Texas for Wallace Campaign headquarters.

"A sign on one of its front windows says, 'Not promoted or financed by the Birch Society.'

" 'We have withdrawn all financial and other support from the American Party, but are still 100 per cent for Wallace, Lewellen says.

"HE AND FOSTER and Steele protest not only what they say is the too-heavy hand of Birchism on the Logan team, but also, what they claim is the personal political opportunism of Logan.

"They say his chief interest now is to use the estimated 6,000 John Birch members in Texas to create a super-structure of control over the estimated 600,000 Wallace followers in Texas — at the expense of the former Alabama governor's presidential run.

"Logan's purpose, the Central Texas trio say; is to build strength for a future Logan candidacy for state-wide office, probably the governorship.

"LEWELLEN SAYS he was ousted from election to the state executive committee in late July by Logan, because Lewellen protested against Birch literature in the Temple headquarters of the American Party, and against the showing of the Birch-produced film, 'Anarchy: USA' in American Party offices.

"Steele resigned the chairmanship of the McLennan County American Party on Aug. 2, as a protest against Logan rulings.

"Foster, now state chairman of the separatist group, tried to hold the contending factions together before the split.

"The dispute is so bitter that the separatists say threats have been made against them and their families.

"THEY HAVE placed the names, political affiliations, and in some cases photos and fingerprints, of those they think are the authors of these threats in four safe deposit boxes in Bell County, Foster says.

"The boxes are to be turned over to police investigating authorities if any effort is made to carry out the threats, he adds.

"All of the dissidents say they have alerted Wallace headquarters in Alabama of the Birch problem. But no real action has been taken yet by the Wallace command there, they say.

"Two men from Wallace's Montgomery, Ala., headquarters, Joe Fine and John DeCarlo, are to meet with the executive committee Monday at the Stephen F. Austin Hotel in Austin. The Birch problem presumably will be aired.

"MRS. MARTEL FORD of Fort Worth, a member of the state executive committee who opposes the Logan tide, says she believes the Alabama governor is keeping hands off because of his conviction on local self-government. He thinks Texans should solve Texas problems, she says.

"Mrs. Ford says she has nothing against Birch Society members, but she feels that Logan has acted unfairly and possibly illegally in deposing elected officials like Lewellen and replacing them with Birch appointees.

"Sidney Beauford of Corpus Christi, who resigned as American Party chairman of the 20th senatorial district, blames over-zealous members of the Birch Society — and not the society as a whole — for the problems that beset the Wallace campaign in Texas.

"BEAUFORD SAYS he was a John Birch member until he quit the society about a year ago, because he disagreed with its political drift them.

"The dissidents feel that things will come to a head at the American Party state convention on Sept. 17 in Dallas. Wallace is to address the convention.

"Logan thinks differently.

" 'It will mainly be a rally for governor, with a minimum of official business,' he says.

"HIS EXPLANATION of the oustings and resignations and other turmoil in the American Party is that it is inevitable in the formation of a new party.

" 'Some fit in, and some don't,' he says.

"Others who haven't 'fitted in' with Logan's plans and have been removed by him are State Secretary Jane Sumner of Austin, State Treasurer Mrs. Margaret Bacon of Austin, and another member of the executive committee, Mrs. Jewell Lemons of San Antonio.

"The dissidents are plainly worried about the surfacing of the Birchers in the Wallace campaign."

Excerpts from the Houston Post — Sunday, November 24, 1968:

"'Wallace in '72' – American Party Builds for Future.

"Still unsettled by the election, however, are the internal problems confronting both the state and county parties. The takeover of the state party by members of the righist John Birch Society still has to be settled, sources in Austin said.

"AND BRYAN admitted late last week his dispute with the factions in the county party still is active.

"'They're still in there – still trying to make trouble and still trying to get at me,' he said."

In 1956 many of the Independent Political Parties, Educational organizations and pressure groups, sent delegates to a meeting in Memphis, for the purpose of establishing a coalition. We understand that $25,000.00 was passed under the table and that was the end of the meeting.

In 1957 Sen. Byrd formed a Senate Finance Investigating Committee to investigate the finances of the nation. He was given the appropriation by Congress. Sens. Jenner, Malone and Kerr were on the Committee. Chairman Byrd stated that the investigation would last from six months to one year. Wm. McChesney Martin, Chairman of Board of the Federal Reserve System, was placed under oath for three weeks. He admitted that "the Government had no right over the Federal Reserve System, except the right of repeal." Ask your Senator for a copy of the proceedings. Then Baruch was put on the stand for a week. All of a sudden the meeting was called to a halt and all committee members declared publicly to the press that they would not run for re-election to the U.S. Senate. The Secret Government had spoken. Read "What's Wrong in Washington" – Omni – 40¢.

On July 24, 1960, Robert Welch, head of the John Birch Society, in a speech held at the Morrison

Hotel, Chicago, Illinois, entitled "To Prevent a Third Party" stated, "The object of this rally, as I understand it, and certainly the purport of what I have to say, is to prevent a third party, not to encourage one."

The John Birch Society has corralled many of our top citizens. However, the top echelon are apparently oblivious of the fact that there is no difference in the two major parties.

In 1962 our State Chairman, Dr. Chas. Finley, endeavored to get us to vote the Republican Ticket and changed or switched our slate of candidates, after we had arranged them for the best interests of the Constitution Party. As a result, only two candidates qualified for ballot position.

In 1963 Bard Logan, President of our Executive Council, resigned from the Constitution Party and joined the American Party. There was more to it than simply a resignation.

In 1963, Bard Logan, President of the Executive Council of the Constitution Party attempted to dissolve the Executive Council. He claimed that he had patent rights on the name Constitution Party. In so doing, he, in effect declared the Constitution Party defunct. He was relying on a registration of the name Constitution Party. Because the officers of the Texas State Executive Committee of the Constitution Party wished to continue use of the name, they, under the advice of counsel, filed a petition with the U.S. Patent Office, to cancel Logan's registration. Over a three-year period, hearings were held, depositions was taken, testimony heard, documents filed, with the result, that it cost the Texas State Executive Committee over $3,000 to obtain cancellation of Logan's registration.

In 1967 there was a "bust-up" in the J.S.B. top echelon.

In 1968, the American Party experienced the same "bust-up" in the top echelon as outlined in the above Houston Post articles. In all of these "bust-ups" it appears that the dedicated Constitutionalists did "come out from among them."

At every turn we have experienced the same undermining tactics by the same group. They apparently have access to unlimited funds. This same situation may exist in other states. We wish to alert the Constitutionalists of every state to be on guard. We implore you to have poll-watchers at all voting machines and computer machines. On the night of November 5th, when the computer "broke down," I told those present, "Good-night, we have been rigged. They are not about to let this election go to the House of Representatives where every State will have one vote." Mechanical devices can be rigged; just like the one-arm bandits.

Daily Intelligencer, Lancaster, Pa. — Nov: 7, 1968.

"Cope Asks FBI Check On Election

"Lloyd G. Cope, Lancaster County chairman of the Constitutional party, said Wednesday that he had filed a formal complaint with the FBI on the conduct Tuesday of the election board at the fourth precinct of the 7th Ward in Lancaster City.

"The complaint alleges that Richard Aspel, a watcher for the Constitutional party, was intimidated and ordered to leave the polling place.

"Cope said that some of the residences claimed by voters were 'vacant lots' and that the clerks voted before filling out voter's cards.

"'It was anything but a fair election,' said Cope, who added there was a widespread movement in other parts of the state to see that the votes for George C. Wallace did not register on the voting machines.

"In Philadelphia, he said, Nelson Fetter, Constitutional party chairman, accompanied by detectives, visited 25 polls and found in 17 of them that the machines would not register a Wallace vote." (End of Quote).

This robbery was Nation-wide.

The following statements were made by General Curtis Lemay, Vice Presidential Candidate, October 30, 1968:

"Curtis LeMay says the American Dollar is in bad shape and George Wallace as President would be the best bookkeeper to straighten it out."

"We're really in bad shape all over the world," LeMay told 300 persons at a $25 a plate dinner last night in Shreveport. "I just wonder about our whole bookkeeping system."

The retired Air Force Chief of Staff said, "Wallace would straighten out the American Dollar at home and abroad."

"I have a suspicion that the money that's being paid into Social Security by taxpayers is being paid out and spent for other things," he said. "I foresee a day of reckoning coming, so I worry about the solvency of the Social Security program." (End of quote).

The following quote was made recently in London, by Roy Jenkins, and reproduced in the New York Times:

"Jenkins' Desire for Reform — London

"Roy Jenkins, Chancellor of the Exchequer, indicated yesterday that it is time to begin considering fundamental reform of the world monetary system.

"The structure of the system is 'wearing a little thin,' he said in calling for an early look at monetary 'objectives' and 'institutions.'

"The Chancellor's remarks were seen as the opening gun in what may become a general movement among the major financial powers. It was certain that he did not make them without taking into consideration opinion in the United States, France and Germany.

"Since the chaos of last week's monetary crisis, many commentators have talked of 'a new Bretton Woods.' But this was the first suggestion from any high monetary official for a radical look at the system, which was created at Bretton Woods, N.H., in 1944.

"Those acquainted with Jenkins' view on the subject do not believe he would favor the calling of a large monetary conference, such as the Bretton Woods meeting, to examine everything from scratch. The effect on monetary conditions, it is thought, would be too unsettling while such a meeting were under way.

"Instead, the idea might be to explore possible reforms quietly with Washington, Paris and Bonn. Only if agreement on a clear plan were seen as possible would a larger conference be called. — New York Times." (End of quote).

Sir Josiah Stamp, second richest man in England, then President of The Bank of England, said, "Take the money creating powers away from the Bankers and all great fortunes like mine will disappear, and they ought to disappear . . . this would then be a better and happier world to live in . . . Banking was conceived in Iniquity and born in Sin." (End of quote).

Four European nations demanded gold for dollars and received I.O.U.s, some bearing 3.5 interest. Congressman Jack Westland asked a Federal Reserve official "how many more non-negotiable I.O.U.s would we be able to sign before a day of reckoning arrived" and was told, "We are getting close to the end of the line right now." — Hearst Headline Service, Special to the Examiner — Washington. (End of quote).

We consider the devaluation of the Pound, Franc and Dollar to be "incidents", to frame the minds of the people, so as to accept the new International Currency, known as Special Drawing Rights(S.D.R.s) or Paper Gold to be put into circulation by the International Monetary Fund and the World Bank.

The following is a quote from the February 1968 "Monthly Review" of the Federal Reserve Bank of Kansas City:

"The annual meeting of the I.M.F. was held in Rio de Janeiro, Brazil, in September 1967, when a resolution was unanimously adopted to proceed with a plan to establish, within the Fund, machinery for the creation of a new international reserve facility." (End of quote).

Apparently, a new International Federal Reserve System is in the making.

The sovereign and inherent right for any government to issue and control its money and credit is more powerful than all other phases of government combined. Any nation that fails to retain this all-powerful right is doomed for the scrap-heap. According to our research, every nation on the face of the earth has un-Constitutionally and without the knowledge and consent of the people, delegated this right to Private Corporations. These Private Monopolies, known as the Bank of England (1694), the Bank of France (1800), and the Federal Reserve System (1913) have strapped the people with indebtedness and interest payments beyond their ability to pay. Simultaneously they have debauched and devalued their currencies. We now have $32 Billion foreign claims against our dwindling gold supply. We anticipate revaluation of gold to $75 per ounce by the International Bankers.

In 1913, when the Federal Reserve Act was introduced, Congressman Lindbergh, of Minnesota, one of the most vocal, said:

"This Act establishes the most gigantic trust on earth. When the President signs the Bill, the invisible Government by the Monetary Power will be legalized . . . The people may not know it immediately, but the day of reckoning is only a few years removed . . . The people must make a declaration of independence to relieve themselves from the monetary power . . . This they will be able to do by taking control of Congress. The division of Congress into political parties is a crime . . ." (End of quote).

"CONGRESSIONAL RECORD — 67th Congress, 4th Session — Senate Document #346 — Justice for Hungary by Mr. LaFollette — 3/3/23

"We repeat, and respectfully submit, that in view of the foregoing facts, it is clearly established that Hungary did not cause and did not bring about the last World War (World War I). The responsibility for the last World War rests solely upon the shoulders of international financiers. It is they upon whose head the blood of millions of dead and millions of dying rests."

"Senate Document #310 — February, 1923

"The famous secret meeting of May 18, 1920, of the Federal Reserve Board, the Federal Reserve Advisory Council and 36 Class 'A' Directors and their agreement secretly made to put on a drastic deflation of credit and currency is notorious." (End of quote).

The deep, dark secret is, who are the Class "A" stockholders of the Federal Reserve System. The FED admit the existance of Class A, B, and C Directors, but only Class B stockholders, who are the Member Banks up and down the Main Streets of America. The Federal Reserve Act gives Congress the option to purchase the Capital Stock of the 12 Federal Reserve Banks, with present assets of $67 Billion for the par value of the outstanding stock which is now $550 Million. There are several bills now in Committee but no one has the stamina to re-introduce them. The Class "C" stock amounts to $150 Million which Congress has the right to purchase, but has never exercised same.

In 1934 Congressman Louis T. McFadden, Chairman of the Banking and Currency Committee said on the floor of the House of Representatives: "Mr. Chairman, we have in this country, one of the most corrupt institutions the world has ever known. I refer to the Federal Reserve Board and the Federal Reserve Banks." . . . (undoubtedly he was referring to the 12 Federal Reserve Banks located in the 12 Federal Reserve Districts — the author) . . . some people think the Federal Reserve Banks are United States Government institutions. They are not Government institutions. They are private monopolies."

Congressman Wright Patman, the present chairman of the Banking and Currency Committee stated, "The two greatest strides in American history are the National Bank Act and the Federal Reserve Act." (They are the very acts which have brought about our un-doing — the author).

U.S. Stand on Money Crisis Assailed — Examiner-London Daily Express — 12-1-68.

An astonishing attack on the American attitude to the recent European currency crisis is made in the ultra-conservative — and normally pro-American — London Economist.

"A blind Martian could find in three minutes a New York banker who is convinced chaos is imminent and inevitable," said the magazine (under the heading, 'And Washington Sleeps On').

"But Treasury Secretary Henry Fowler is essentially expressing the view that nothing fundamental is wrong with the system and that nothing fundamental is needed by way of reform."

If this Washington view prevails, warns the Economist, the world will lurch blindly into another money crisis.

In the leading article, the theme is pursued with bitter cynicism.

"'The outgoing Administration,' said the writer, 'has been passionately opposed in its last days to any currency being devalued anywhere for fear that it posed a threat to the dollar.'

"That was why President Johnson was prevailed on by his officials to send that fulsome telegraph of congratulations to President de Gaulle when the old man decided to ignore realities for a little while longer by sticking to his overvalued rate.

"It is likely, the article goes on, that when President Nixon arrives in Washington he will delay advance towards reform until the next international crisis.

"Fowler is described as 'a dead duck' bolstered by the inactivity of the British government, which should, the Economist says, have taken an initiative in forcing the pace towards more flexible exchange rates.

"The gloomy conclusion is that there will be two more Bonn meetings before a monetary catastrophe occurs." (End of London Daily Express quote).

FLASH! December 27th, 1968 was the Second Declaration of Independence. On that momentous date, and for the first time in the history of this nation, a judge and jury decreed that creation of credit by bookkeeping entries by Commercial Banks was un-Constitutional, and null and void. Following is the resume and Memorandum of the case in question.

STATE OF MINNESOTA
COUNTY OF SCOTT

IN JUSTICE COURT
TOWNSHIP OF CREDIT RIVER
MARTIN V. MAHONEY, JUSTICE

First National Bank of Montgomery,
Plantiff,

vs. **JUDGE & DECREE**

Jerome Daly, **Defendant.**

The above entitled action came on before the Court and a Jury of 12 on December 7, 1968 at 10:00 A.M. Plaintiff appeared by its President Lawrence V. Morgan and was represented by its Counsel Theodore R. Mellby. Defendant appeared on his own behalf.

A Jury of Talesmen were called, impanneled and sworn to try the issues in this Case. Lawrence V. Morgan was the only witness called for Plaintiff and Defendant testified as the only witness in his own behalf.

Plaintiff brought this as a Common Law action for the recovery of the possession of Lot 19, Fairview Beach, Scott County, Minn. Plaintiff claimed titled to the Real Property in question by foreclosure of a Note and Mortgage Deed dated May 8, 1964 which Plaintiff claimed was in default at the time foreclosure proceedings were started.

Defendant appeared and answered that the Plaintiff created the money and credit upon its own books by bookkeeping entry as the consideration for the Note and Mortgage of May 8, 1964 and alleged failure of consideration for the Mortgage Deed and alleged that the Sheriff's sale passed no title to Plaintiff.

The issues tried to the Jury were whether there was a lawful consideration and whether Defendant had waived his rights to complain about the consideration having paid on the Note for almost 3 years.

Mr. Morgan admitted that all of the money or credit which was used as a consideration was created upon their books, that this was standard banking practice exercised by their bank in combination with the Federal Reserve Bank of Minneapolis, another private Bank, further that he knew of no United States Statute or Law that gave the Plaintiff the authority to do this. Plaintiff further claimed that Defendant by using the ledger book created credit and by paying on the Note and Mortgage waived any right to complain about the Consideration and that Defendant was estopped from doing so.

At 12:15 on December 7, 1968 the Jury returned a unanimous verdict for the Defendant.

Now therefore, by virture of the authority vested in me pursuant to the Declaration of Independence, the Northwest Ordinance of 1787, the Constitution of the United States and the Constitution and laws of the State of Minnesota not inconsistent therewith;

IT IS HEREBY ORDERED, ADJUDGED & DECREED:

1. That Plaintiff is not entitled to recover the possession of Lot 19, Fairview Beach, Scott County, Minnesota according to the Plat thereof on file in the Register of Deeds office.

2. That because of failure of a lawful consideration the Note and Mortgage dated May 8, 1964 are null and void.

3. That the Sheriff's sale of the above described premises held on June 26, 1967 is null and void, of no effect.

4. That Plaintiff has no right, title or interest in said premises or lien thereon, as is above described.

5. That any provision in the Minnesota Constitution and any Minnesota Statute limiting the Jurisdiction of this Court is repugnant to the Constitution of the United States and to the Bill of Rights of the Minnesota Constitution and is null and void and that this Court has Jurisdiction to render complete Justice in this Cause.

6. That Defendant is awarded costs in the sum of $75.00 and execution is hereby issued therefore.

7. A 10 day stay is granted.

8. The following memorandum and any supplemental memorandum made and filed by this Court in support of this Judgment is hereby made a part hereof by reference.

BY THE COURT

Dated December 9, 1968

MARTIN V. MAHONEY
JUSTICE OF THE PEACE
CREDIT RIVER TOWNSHIP
SCOTT COUNTY, MINNESOTA

MEMORANDUM

The issues in this case were simple. There was no material dispute on the facts for the Jury to resolve.

Plaintiff admitted that it, in combination with the Federal Reserve Bank of Minneapolis, which are for all practical purposes, because of there interlocking activity and practices, and both being Banking Institutions Incorporated under the Laws of the United States, are in the Law to be treated as one and the same Bank, did create the entire $14,000.00 in money or credit upon its own books by bookkeeping entry. That this was the Consideration used to

support the Note dated May 8, 1964 and the Mortgage of the same date. The money and credit first came into existance when they created it. Mr. Morgan admitted that no United States Law or Statute existed which gave him the right to do this. A lawful consideration must exist and be tendered to support the Note. See Anheuser-Busch Brewing Co. v. Emma Mason, 44 Minn. 318, 46 N.W. 558. The Jury found there was no lawful consideration and I agree. Only God can create something of value out of nothing.

Even if Defendant could be charged with waiver or estoppel as a matter of Law this is no defense to the Plaintiff. The Law leaves wrongdoers where it finds them. See sections 50, 51 and 52 of Am Jur 2d "Actions" on page 584 — "no action will lie to recover on a claim based upon, or in any manner depending upon, a fraudulent, illegal, or immoral transaction or contract to which Plaintiff was a party."

Plaintiff's act of creating credit is not authorized by the Constitution and Laws of the United States, is unconstitutional and void, and is not a lawful consideration in the eyes of the Law to support any thing or upon which any lawful rights can be built.

Nothing in the Constitution of the United States limits the Jurisdiction of this Court, which is one of original Jurisdiction with right of trial by Jury guaranteed. This is a Common Law Action. Minnesota cannot limit or impair the power of this Court to render Complete Justice between the parties. Any provisions in the Constitution and laws of Minnesota which attempt to do so is repugnant to the Constitution of the United States and is void. No question as to the Jurisdiction of this Court was raised by either party at the trial. Both paries were given complete liberty to submit any and all facts and law to the Jury, at least in so far as they saw fit.

No complaint was made by Plaintiff that Plaintiff did not receive a fair trial. From the admissions made by Mr. Morgan the path of duty was made direct and clear for the Jury. Their Verdict could not reasonably have been otherwise. Justice was rendered completely and without denial, promptly and without delay, freely and without purchase, conformable to the laws in this Court on December 7, 1968.

BY THE COURT

December 9, 1968

/S/ MARTIN V. MAHONEY
JUSTICE OF THE PEACE
CREDIT RIVER TOWNSHIP
SCOTT COUNTY, MINNESOTA

Note: It has never been doubted that a Note given on a Consideration is prohibited by law is void. It has been determined, independent of Acts of Congress, that sailing under the license of an enemy is illegal. The emmission of Bills of Credit upon the books of these private Corporations, for the purposes of private gain is not warranted by the Constitution of the United States and is unlawful. See Craig v. Mo. 4 Peters Reports 912. This Court can tread only that path which is marked out by duty. M.V.M.

For further details write to:

THE MINNESOTA ACTION FUND
628 Stryker Avenue
St. Paul, Minnesota 55107

St. John 2:15—"*And when he had made a scourge of small cords, he drove them all out of the temple, and the sheep, and the oxen, and poured out the changers' money, and over-threw the tables.*"

1 Timothy 5:10—"*FOR THE LOVE of money is the root of all evil: which while some coveted after, they have erred from the faith, and pierced themselves through with many sorrows.*"

In His Name,
WICKLIFFE B. VENNARD, SR.
National Chairman
Americans For America
P.O. Box 13238
HOUSTON, TEXAS 77019

• • •

CODE

I.B.s—International Bankers
J.B.s—John Birch Society
FRS—Federal Reserve System
FED—Federal Reserve System
CFR—Council on Foreign Relations
IMF—International Monetary Fund

Books by the same author.

Titles:	One Copy	Ten Copies
"Conquest or Consent"	$2.00	$10.50
"The Federal Reserve Hoax"	2.00	12.50
"What's Wrong in Washington?"	.40	2.00
"The Enemy Within"	.25	1.50
"50 Years of Treason"	.25	1.50
"Solution to the Federal Reserve Fraud"	.25	1.50
"World War III Shaping Up"	.10	1.00
"Chronological History of United States Money	.25	1.50
"U. S. Rulers Are Undiscoverable"	.25	1.50